EXPLOITING THE SEA

Malcolm Penny

The Bookwright Press
New York • 1991

Titles in this series

Exploiting the Sea
Exploring the Sea
Food from the Sea
Life in the Sea
The Ocean Floor
Waves, Tides and Currents

First published in the
United States in 1991 by
The Bookwright Press
387 Park Avenue South
New York, NY 10016

First published in 1990 by
Wayland (Publishers) Ltd
61 Western Road, Hove
East Sussex BN3 1JD, England

Library of Congress Cataloging-in-Publication Data
Penny, Malcolm.
p. cm. — (The Sea)
Includes bibliographical references and index.
Summary: Discusses the human uses of the sea (source of food, means of
travel), the human effect on the sea, and the protection of the sea and its
treasures.
ISBN 0–531–18359–9
1. Marine resources—Juvenile literature. [1. Marine resources. 2. Marine
pollution. 3. Pollution. 4. Marine resources conservation. 5. Man—Influence
on nature.] I. Title. II. Series: Penny, Malcolm. Sea.
GC 1016.5.P46   1991
333.91′64—dc20   90–38112
CIP
AC

Phototypeset by Rachel Gibbs, Wayland
Printed in Italy by L.E.G.O. S.p.A., Vicenza

CONTENTS

An oil rig in the North Sea. This rig could endanger waters that are an important source of food for many Europeans.

THE GENEROUS SEA

The vast expanse of ocean, with all its power and its unpredictable moods, must have seemed very frightening to our ancestors. No wonder many early peoples worshiped the sea as a god, making sacrifices to it in the hope that it would spare their lives and provide them with food. The produce of the generous sea was regarded as a gift from nature.

In ancient times, people exploited the sea for food, but only near the shore, in shallow water. Shells found in the refuse dumps of prehistoric settlements indicate that early people ate shellfish. They must certainly have eaten seaweed, some forms of which are still used as food today. Later, people used traps and nets to catch fish near the shore.

Today, food from the sea is often treated as though it were an endless resource. This has caused many problems, including over-fishing. Modern fishing boats, which have powerful engines and freezers on board, can travel great distances and stay at sea for a long time. Some fisheries are so efficient that they are in danger of wiping out whole fish populations.

Whaling has followed the same course. When it began a few whales were killed one at a time with primitive weapons, but now factory ships have killed so many

Top Indonesians fishing with nets from the shore. This type of fishing does not harm fish populations. *Below* Seaweed being collected for use as fertilizer.

whales that some species may never recover their numbers. Turtles and seals were killed for food, oil, shells and skins, until they, too, were almost wiped out.

The sea provides more than food. It is a source of minerals such as salt, which we use both to season and preserve our food. Sea water is used to cool power stations; the waves and tides are used to generate electricity.

Sad to say, some people still treat the ocean as though it has an unlimited capacity to provide food and resources and, at the same time, to cope with society's wastes. In the past, when there were far fewer people to exploit the sea, and wastes were less poisonous, the sea did not seem to suffer from human abuses. Now we know that we are capable of causing permanent damage to the sea. We also know that this would be the most disastrous mistake of all, because the sea is vitally important to life on this planet.

Fur seals were once hunted all over the world, until there were very few left. Now that they are protected, many populations have recovered.

THE SEA AS A HIGHWAY

Sailing ships like this East Indiaman once carried passengers and goods all over the world, doing no harm to the sea.

Long ago, people learned to make boats and travel on the sea. People from the South Pacific islands sailed enormous distances to New Zealand and Madagascar. Later, the Vikings sailed from Scandinavia to Iceland and Greenland, and even to North America, long before Christopher Columbus.

The early canoes and sailing boats, and even the coal-fired steamers of the nineteenth century, left no sign of their passing on the surface of the sea. Sometimes boats sank or were washed up on shore, but they did almost no damage to the sea itself.

The travels of early explorers caused some changes to sea life. Seaweeds were carried to places where they had never grown before, and the dreaded shipworm traveled from the Atlantic into the Pacific, on the hulls of the first wooden ships to round Cape Horn at the southern tip of South America. Shipworms burrow into timber, leaving large holes that can eventually cause a ship to break up.

When oil-fired ships were invented, they brought a new problem with them: oil pollution.

Opposite A nuclear-powered submarine can stay under the sea for months at a time, hidden from enemies. However, if it is ever involved in an accident, its fuel could be very dangerous.

Until the 1960s, most people traveled from one country to another by sea, in ocean liners that were like huge floating hotels. The liners spilled oil wherever they went, usually in quite small quantities, but enough to do some damage. Even small gasoline-driven outboard motorboats cause pollution in enclosed harbors.

Although people now usually travel by air, a great deal of cargo, especially oil, still goes by sea. It has become all too common to hear of accidents in which giant oil tankers have spilled their cargo, polluting large areas of sea and shore and causing the deaths of birds, fish and other animals. Some large ships carry chemical and nuclear waste, with the ever-present risk that a storm or a collision might cause them to spill their poisonous cargo into the water.

A new danger to the sea is the nuclear-powered submarine. These submarines are an amazing advancement in shipping technology; they are able to stay underwater almost indefinitely, without refueling. However, if one of these vessels is wrecked, dangerous fuel might be released into the sea causing untold damage.

For more than a hundred years, ocean liners were the main form of transportation between continents. Now, they are used mainly for cruises.

DUMPING WASTES AT SEA

The sea has always been used as a dumping ground for waste of all kinds. In the past, wastes were mostly natural substances, such as offal and sewage, and they were dumped in relatively small amounts. These types of waste were easily dispersed throughout the sea, and marine life could even feed on them. The damage was not serious, though some fish and shellfish, caught close to shores polluted by sewage, were probably not very safe to eat.

The waste in the sea now is very different, and it arrives in much greater quantities. Industrial waste containing poisonous chemicals and heavy metals is dumped into rivers that flow into the sea. Pesticides and fertilizers wash off farmland and down the same rivers into the sea. A large amount of sewage is still being released untreated into the sea, even by industrially advanced nations such as Britain. Pollutants enter the water when toxic wastes are burned at sea; other pollutants literally fall from the sky when rain washes out solid particles in the smoke from industrial chimneys.

The type of damage caused by dumping at sea depends on the

types of waste. Toxic inorganic waste poisons living things; in contrast, organic waste, especially nitrates and fertilizers, encourages plant growth. But this can lead to a serious problem known as eutrophication, meaning "overfeeding," which causes algae in the sea to grow very quickly. Such sudden growth is called an "algal bloom." When the algae die, the

A pied wagtail feeding by the outlet of a sewage pipe. Many animals live quite happily in such conditions, but so do germs.

A river in England, heavily polluted by wastes from a tin mine.

Factories are essential for modern life, but the waste chemicals and smoke they produce create problems for the environment.

bacteria that feed on them remove much of the oxygen from the water. As a result, fish and other marine life may be starved of oxygen and die.

The North Sea is one of the most polluted seas in the world. Rivers from the industrial countries of Western and Central Europe flow into the southern part of the North Sea, where the main currents, which move counter-clockwise, carry their burden of pollution toward the coast of the Continent. It is not surprising that the main demand to reduce the pollution in the North Sea comes from West Germany. Britain may be able to get rid of its wastes on currents moving away from its shore, but they all flow toward Germany.

Raw sewage flowing across a beach in New Zealand, close to a popular surfing area.

HARMFUL CHANGES TO THE SEA

To many animals, the sea is not only their home but also a trusted friend whose regular seasonal changes serve to regulate their lives. Human interference can alter this, turning the sea into a death-trap. One such change to the sea is known as thermal pollution.

Thermal pollution occurs when water that has been used for cooling in power stations is pumped back into the sea, much

Some litter is dropped by careless vacationers, and some is washed in from the sea: it all spoils the pleasure of a day on the beach.

warmer than when it was taken out. This often changes the living patterns of sea creatures. For example, there are now animals and plants living near the nuclear power stations in the Severn Estuary in Britain whose real home is in the warmer waters of the Mediterranean.

Off the coast of Florida, the manatees, which normally move inland to warm springs for the winter, now stay out at sea, basking in the warm outflows from the power stations. If a power station has to be shut down for any reason in the winter, the manatees become ill and die in the cold water.

Most people do not notice what has happened to the ocean until

Left Manatees in Florida bask in the warm water coming from the cooling system of a power station. They are safe until the power station has to be closed down.

they go to the beach for vacation. In 1989, an algal bloom off the coast of Yugoslavia spoiled many holidays. Although it was reported that this particular bloom was not poisonous, people on vacation in northern Yugoslavia were faced with a sea covered with thick gray slime. The bloom was caused by agricultural chemicals that had flowed into the sea.

Oil, swept ashore from the sea, can be found on most beaches. Hotels and guest houses at the shore often have notices asking people to remove oil from their feet before coming inside. On some beaches, it is not safe to walk barefoot because of all the dangerous rubbish that has been washed up.

Once, the most dangerous creatures in the ocean were great white sharks or poisonous jellyfish; today, the dangerous creatures are much smaller. Tiny bacteria and viruses from sewage discharges at sea can cause serious and even fatal diseases.

Plastic bottles can be seen floating among the driftwood and cuttlefish bones. Even on remote islands, rubber shoes and polystyrene packing materials litter beaches that are hundreds of miles away from regular shipping lanes. All these changes to the sea environment are most unpleasant and are often very dangerous.

This beach has been swamped with oil from a tanker accident. Even beaches that look clean often have tarry lumps of oil on them.

Nuclear power stations, like this one on Lake Ontario in Canada, change the living conditions for animals living in the water, usually by warming it up.

OIL AND WATER DO NOT MIX

Right A dead gannet soaked in oil. Even small amounts of oil can poison birds or ruin their feathers.

In March 1989, the giant oil tanker *Exxon Valdez* hit a rock in Prince William Sound, in Alaska. It spilled millions of gallons of crude oil into the waters of one of the least-spoiled bays in the world. It was the worst tanker disaster ever to happen in North America, and one of the worst in the world. This was just the latest in a long series of oil spills, all of them the result of exploiting the sea as a highway on which to carry large and dangerous cargoes.

Oil harms animals in different ways. Birds lose the use of their feathers when they become clogged with oil; the birds cannot fly or keep warm. Mammals, too, find that their oil-matted fur no longer insulates them from the cold. When they try to clean themselves, the animals swallow the oil, which burns their stomachs and eventually damages their livers and kidneys. If they breathe the fumes drifting across the water, their lungs are damaged. Almost all the animals exposed to the oil will die.

There is another, and much longer-lasting, effect of oil pollution. Oil is a mixture of many chemicals, some of them light and others heavy. The lightest components of the oil dissolve in the water, poisoning tiny animals in the plankton, as

Leaked oil surrounds the wrecked tanker Exxon Valdez *off the coast of Alaska.*

well as the fish that eat them. The heavier chemicals sink to the bottom, where they form a poisonous blanket over animals and plants that live on the sea-bed. These effects will persist long after the last bird or mammal has died, or been cleaned and treated. It may be many years before the food chain can grow up again in an area that has been badly affected by an oil spill.

The ocean is also at constant risk from accidents to oil rigs or the wells far below them on the sea-bed. Oil drilled from the

bottom of the sea is not a natural product of the sea itself. It comes from ancient land that is now submerged. When there is a spill at sea, attempts are made to scoop up the oil or to disperse it using chemicals. However, these chemicals are often more poisonous than the oil itself. The only safe solution is to prevent accidents and to stop the deliberate dumping of oil at sea.

Above When an underwater well leaked in the Gulf of Mexico, the spread of pollution was limited by burning the oil at the surface.

Left Cleaning oil from the shore with detergent, after the tanker *Torrey Canyon* was wrecked in the English Channel.

13

RECLAIMING LAND FROM THE SEA

Another way of exploiting the sea is to drain shallow places around its edges to make new land. This practice is called reclaiming the land. Drainage from the sea-bed to make land was pioneered by the people of the Netherlands, much of whose country is below sea level. By digging canals and building banks of earth, or dikes, they were able to create farmland from the bottom of the sea. The areas of land created in this way are known as polders.

When the Zuider Zee was drained in 1932, several large polders were created and a large area of salt water was closed off from the sea and allowed to become a freshwater lake. This might truly be called reclamation because this area of land had been flooded by the North Sea in the thirteenth century. After the flooding, salt-water animals invaded the Zuider Zee. But when the area was reclaimed, these creatures died out as the water gradually became less salty and finally fresh. Herrings, anchovies and plaice, which had once provided food for people as well as a large population of seals, disappeared, as did the seals themselves. But one species of crab survived, along with an acorn barnacle, as a reminder that the Zuider Zee was once part of the North Sea.

Much smaller operations, such as building harbors or sea walls, also affect the sea nearby. By changing the currents and reducing the effect of wave action, they alter the movements of sand and mud on the sea-bed close to the shore. This can

The canals in the Netherlands were dug in order to drain land for farming. They became beautiful highways across the country, used for trade and pleasure.

reduce or remove altogether the habitats of animals such as ragworms and shellfish that burrow in sand and mud. These small animals are the main food of wading birds such as redshanks, dunlin and curlews, Some of the birds migrate over long distances, and they rely on large muddy areas with plenty of food as stopping places on their journeys. In this way, even minor building activities in one country can have harmful consequences for birds from far away.

The Florida Keys are a chain of small islands stretching south from the tip of Florida into the Gulf of Mexico. Over the years, people have built bridges and causeways to join the islands by road. These structures have created new currents, which in turn have washed away much of the sand and mud that was the habitat for many small sea creatures that once lived in the shallow waters between the islands.

Below One of the bridges connecting the Florida Keys is about 7 miles (11 km) long. The bridge supports have altered the sea currents, and mud and sand have been washed away.

POWER FROM THE SEA

Anyone who watches the tides ebb and flow cannot fail to be impressed by the huge amounts of water on the move, particularly in a narrow inlet such as an estuary. In some estuaries the tide comes in as a single large wave, called a bore.

Electricity can be generated by using falling water to turn turbines, often by damming a river or diverting a waterfall through pipes. The same thing can be done with large estuaries, using the movements of the tides. A dam, or barrage, with turbines inside is built across the mouth of the estuary. As the tide ebbs and flows past the barrage, it turns the turbines.

The sea roars through the barrage on the Rance River, in Brittany, France, as the tide comes in. This power turns turbines to generate electricity.

There is a huge barrage in the Bay of Fundy, in Newfoundland, Canada, which has the greatest tidal range in the world. At spring tides, the difference between high and low water is well over 33 feet (10 m). The second highest tidal range is almost as great, in the Severn Estuary, between England and Wales. There is currently a plan to build a barrage there too.

A barrage generates electricity without causing pollution, but it can cause other problems. The Bay of Fundy barrage lies across one small arm of the huge estuary, but the Severn barrage would cut the whole estuary off from the sea. Where shorebirds now feed on mudbanks at low tide, the whole area would be permanently underwater. In the salt marshes created by winter floods grasses grow that are food for flocks of migrating geese. If the barrage were to be built, the water level would be controlled so that winter floods would no longer happen; and there would never be another Severn bore.

The lake created by a barrage might be wonderful for those people who like water sports, but a great deal of wildlife would suffer. The Severn is an important river for breeding eels and salmon. There would be a salmon ladder to allow the fish to get into the river, but the currents would be changed by the barrage. The

water temperature would change as well, because the warm water from the cooling towers of the two nuclear power stations would take longer to escape to the sea.

Other ways of generating electricity are to make use of waves and currents in the sea itself. But so far, these techniques are only in an experimental stage.

Above In England the Severn bore sweeps up the river when the tide rises.

The Bay of Fundy, in Newfoundland, Canada, has the largest tidal range in the world.

FISH FROM THE SEA

Catching fish involves hunting them from a wild population. This is quite different from raising animals for meat or breeding stock. Modern fisheries have become so efficient that it is now possible to wipe out whole fish populations, so there is no breeding stock left in the wild.

Not long ago, there were so few herrings left in the North Sea that it was not worth fishing for them. Then the fishery stopped, and gradually the remaining herrings bred a new population. The herring fishermen learned that sustainable exploitation is only possible if the numbers and size of fish that are caught are carefully controlled.

If fishermen know the minimum size a fish must be before it can breed, they can make sure that fishing nets have a mesh wide enough to allow fish of this size to escape. The fishing fleet can return to catch the fish the next year, after they have had a chance to breed. In this way, fisheries are able to maintain sustainable catches.

Fishing methods that use suction pipes instead of nets cannot control the size of fish

"Fly nets" to catch salmon on a tidal river in Scotland. The fish "fly" in at high tide, then at low tide the nets can be emptied.

they take and can seriously reduce fish populations. In the South Atlantic, along the edge of the Antarctic Ocean, fishing boats from the USSR and Japan are sucking up millions of tons of fish. No one has yet studied the fish populations in the area to find out how many fish there are and how quickly they can breed. Unless these fishing activities are controlled, the South Atlantic may soon be over-fished.

In the Shetland Islands between 1984 and 1988, some seabirds produced very few young. This disaster happened because commercial fishing for sand eels had wiped out the birds' main food source. Most of the one-year-old fish normally eaten by the adult birds were taken, as well as the tiny first-year fish needed by the chicks. Sand eels cannot breed until they are two years old. The fishery was not only

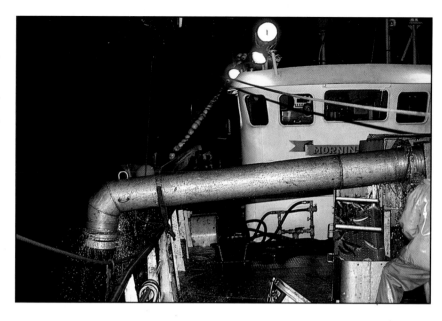

starving the birds, it was also destroying the sand eel breeding stock. In 1982, the sand eel catch was 57,900 tons; by 1988, only 5,300 tons were caught. Clearly, the fishery was being destroyed by over-fishing. In 1989, the sand eel fishery was closed, but it will be many years before the populations of birds and fish recover.

When fishermen take fish from the sea with pumps, they cannot control what size of fish they catch. This can harm the fish population.

Puffins need plenty of sand eels to eat, especially during the breeding season when they are feeding their chicks.

THE TRAGEDY OF WHALING

The worst example of over-exploitation of a stock of wild animals has been the destruction of the great whales. For at least a thousand years, whalers in small boats used hand-held harpoons. They took only one whale at a time, and the damage to the whale population was quite small. When whaling developed into an industry, early in the twentieth century, the damage was catastrophic.

Factory ships sailed the whaling grounds, each served by a fleet of fast boats armed with guns that fired exploding harpoons. The catchers towed their victims to the factory and then set out to kill more whales. In the 1960s, the whaling industry was killing over 60,000 whales every year. Even in 1972, more than 40,000 whales were killed.

There were probably about 250,000 blue whales and 300,000 humpback whales before whaling began. The survivors of each species now number approximately 10,000 to 12,000. With the decline in the numbers of large whales, the countries that continued whaling, principally the USSR and Japan, had to hunt smaller whales. Between 1974 and 1989, they greatly reduced the number of fin whales.

The industry was destroying the stocks that it needed in order to survive. In 1972, the United Nations declared a temporary ban on whaling. This is giving scientists an opportunity to study

A sperm whale being dragged ashore in the Azores. Another in the background is being cut up.

whale populations to find out if they can be hunted in a sustainable way, but it may be too late for some of the larger species of whales to recover to their original numbers. There are now so few left in the sea that they may simply not meet other whales often enough to breed. But there is another problem facing the whales – increasing competition for their food supply.

The main food of the great whales is a shrimp-like creature called krill. As the whale population was being reduced and, therefore, eating fewer krill, other sea animals who eat krill began to grow in numbers. For example, fur seals who were hunted close to extinction, have almost fully recovered their numbers. Crabeater seals now breed at an earlier age, an indication that they are getting much more to eat. Macaroni penguins are also multiplying faster than usual. As these animals increase in numbers,

they will continue to eat more krill. In addition, a growing human krill fishery takes millions of tons from the sea each year. All this competition to catch krill means less food for the great whales.

Top Freshly caught krill. The biggest of these shrimplike animals are about 1 inch (2.5 cm) long.

Lower Macaroni penguins eat only krill. A colony of 100,000 birds needs 180 tons per day when they are feeding their chicks.

Left A sperm whale breaching near the Galapagos Islands.

GIFTS FROM THE SEA

Many shells from tropical reefs have very attractive colors and interesting shapes. Collecting them was once a popular hobby, and some of them are still worth a great deal of money. The shiny, patterned shell of the cowrie has been a favorite among collectors. The beautiful shell of this snail-like creature has evolved for specific purposes. It is thick to protect the cowrie from the powerful jaws of crabs and fish. There is a thin skin covering the shell that allows the cowrie to breathe. When the cowrie is alarmed, it quickly withdraws its skin inside its shell. The smooth shiny surface of its shell allows it to do this. Once the skin has been withdrawn, the patterns and colors on the shell help to camouflage the cowrie.

Coral jewelry, mother-of-pearl ornaments and tortoiseshell frames for eyeglasses are all made from parts of tropical sea animals. Coral is the mass of limestone tubes made by tiny animals for shelter. Mother-of-pearl is the smooth lining that seasnails lay down inside their shells. Tortoiseshell is the shell of the hawksbill turtle, now very rare because it has been over-hunted.

Even the round sea-sponge, which some people use to wash with, was once the home of a group of living animals.

Harvesting all these materials involves killing the animals that made them. Collecting live shells often means breaking up the reefs where they hide. As the reefs are destroyed, all the thousands of other creatures that live on them – colorful fish of all shapes

Shells for sale on a stall in the Seychelles, a few years ago. Collecting shells among the islands is now banned by law.

and sizes, sea urchins, crabs, and many others – are made homeless. The coral may take many years to rebuild.

However, in more and more places local people have realized that a colorful, undamaged reef attracts tourists. Snorkeling over reefs has become an essential part of many tropical vacations, and consequently, many reefs are now strictly protected. There are plenty of dead shells and wave-washed pieces of coral on beaches for people to collect; but in many countries the protection is now so strict that even these must be left where they are.

The shell of a hawksbill turtle is covered with beautiful plates of "tortoiseshell." The turtles are now rare because they have been hunted for their shells, to make ornaments.

Sponges collected from the sea are soft and absorbent, and very good for washing with; but they were once the home of colonies of small animals.

SALT AND WATER FROM THE SEA

One obvious product from the sea is salt. In some places, for example in San Francisco Bay, making salt from sea water is a major industry. Large shallow ponds, or saltpans, lie in the sun, and as the water gradually evaporates, the salt is left behind. It is a slow process. The water is moved from pond to pond through pumps and sluices, getting saltier at each stage, until finally only the salt is left. It takes five years to evaporate 5,800 gallons (22,000 litres) of sea water to produce 1 ton of salt. The San Francisco salt works can produce 1 million tons per year.

Bulldozers scrape the salt into heaps, and it is taken away to be purified. A small amount of salt is an important part of everyone's diet, and many people think that sea salt is healthier to eat than other kinds.

While the water is evaporating, it can be used to breed brine shrimps, which grow well in very salty water. They are then collected up to be used as fish food for aquariums.

Making salt sounds like a harmless way of exploiting the sea, but in some places it has caused damage to the environment and harmed some very rare animals. In San Francisco Bay, saltpans cover over 62 square miles (160 sq km) of the shore. Building them has meant destroying the existing salt marshes and all the plants and animals that lived in them. In San Francisco Bay, a bird called the California clapper rail and the salt marsh harvest mouse have become almost extinct because they have lost so much of their habitat.

Other chemicals are extracted from sea water, including phosphates and nitrates to be used as fertilizer, and magnesium and bromine to be used in industry. There is silver and gold

Wherever the sun is hot enough, evaporating seawater to make salt is big business. But creating salt-pans destroys the habitat of many shallow-water animals.

in sea water, too, but in such small quantities that it would cost more to extract the metals than they are worth.

Another obvious product of the sea is drinking water. In many countries where fresh water is in short supply, the only way to provide water for people to drink is to take it from the sea. All the salt must be removed before the water can be used, and this process of desalination uses up a great deal of energy.

Collecting salt in San Francisco Bay. Fourteen of these giant tractors, working together, can collect 350 tons of salt in one hour.

Removing the salt from sea water provides an important source of drinking water for people living in desert countries.

FARMING A CLEAN SEA

A clean sea could be a valuable source of food for the whole human race. Fish is an excellent source of food. Some fish are inedible because they produce poisons to protect themselves from predators. The puffer fish, or fugu, in the waters off Japan is one example; but even it can be eaten if all the poisonous parts are removed by a skillfull chef. However, there are fish in all parts of the world that have been made poisonous by living in water that has been polluted by human activities. Sewage and pesticides can make fish dangerous to eat. Heavy metals, especially mercury from industrial wastes, can become absorbed into fish, turning them from a safe food into a deadly meal.

Oysters have been grown in special beds in Japan for over two hundred years, and in Europe for over a century. Many other shellfish can be grown in the same way, and they are a very good source of food. Two and a half acres (1 hectare) of the best

Kelp is discharged at the dockside at San Diego, California. Kelp is a valuable food product but, if it is to be fit for human consumption, it must be harvested from a clean sea.

grassland can produce 250 pounds (114 kg) of beef each year, but the same area of shellfish bed can produce over 12 tons of "meat" – one hundred times as much as the grasslands. Although beef provides more energy per pound, the shellfish bed produces over six times as much energy as a field of the same size. However, the shellfish are only as safe as the water they live in. If the water is polluted, so are the shellfish.

Rearing marine fish in captivity is quite a new industry. So far, rearing salmon has been most successful. Nevertheless, problems arise because the fish have to be kept in crowded conditions in cages. Disease can spread quickly, and the droppings of the fish can cause eutrophication of nearby water, with all the problems that can bring.

A large seaweed called kelp is very valuable as a food additive and for many other uses, including making toothpaste and beer that stays frothy! Kelp grows very fast, so it can be harvested regularly. For thousands of years, people have collected other types of seaweed from beaches to use as food.

All these foods from the sea are only as healthy as the sea itself. In order to farm the sea safely, we must first have water that is clean and unpolluted.

SAVING THE SEA

We exploit the sea for its food and resources, and we use it to ship goods from one land mass to another. However, while we use the sea for our present purposes, we must also protect it for future generations. Sea pollution has reached such a high level that if we are to save the sea, we must act now.

In recent years, we have come to understand more fully how human activities affect the sea's complex environmental system. For example, the traces of pesticides found in penguins in the Antarctic show that pollution spreads everywhere. The sea is no place to get rid of nuclear waste or toxic chemicals, no matter how deep they are buried. We can no longer afford to use the sea as a dump for our waste materials or treat it as an endless resource for exploitation.

At present we depend on oil as a vital energy source. Until safer energy alternatives are found, we

We all need oil for fuel, but moving it across the oceans in large tankers is a risky business.

For our distant ancestors, the sea, for all its terrifying power and mystery, was also a beautiful and bountiful gift of nature. They could wander on beaches that were free of oil and plastic litter; they could hunt in a sea full of fish that were safe to eat; and they could watch in awe the magnificent whales, blowing in the sparkling waters. If we use our understanding of the sea to prevent further pollution and over-exploitation, future generations will once again be able to enjoy the benefits of a clean and unpolluted sea.

will continue to ship oil from one country to another. Whatever the cost, we must make sure that ships carrying oil are safe enough to prevent spillage.

Fishing can be sustainable, as long as we take only a certain number before the fish have a chance to recover by breeding.

As the human population grows, so does the amount of waste that it produces. The proper treatment of sewage and the disposal of factory waste are the responsibilities of governments; but there are other ways in which individuals can reduce the damage to the sea. Using biodegradable detergents and pesticides that break down quickly is a choice all people can make each time they go shopping. If people refuse to buy environmentally harmful products, they are less likely to appear in the stores.

Left Clean seas provide food and support wildlife; and clean, safe beaches provide happy places for vacations.

The sea provided a life-supporting environment for animals long before humans appeared on the planet. We owe it to ourselves and our descendants, and to all the animals that depend on the sea, to keep the oceans healthy and unpolluted.

GLOSSARY

Algae Simple plants, ranging from very small to seaweed.

Bacteria Tiny one-celled creatures that cause decay. Some bacteria cause disease.

Barnacle A small shellfish that attaches itself to rocks, wharves, ships' bottoms etc. in the sea.

Barrage An artificial obstruction in a watercourse.

Biodegradable Capable of breaking down naturally into substances that do not harm the environment.

Camouflage To take on a disguise by appearing to be part of the surroundings.

Causeway An artificial strip of land connecting an island to the shore.

Cuttlefish A ten-armed, squid-like mollusk. Its body is supported by a chalky central "bone."

Ebb and flow The receding and advancing of the tide.

Estuary The place where a river widens out when it reaches the sea.

Eutrophication Over-feeding; when it happens in the sea, eutrophication can cause too much plant growth and consequent loss of oxygen.

Exploitation The act of taking advantage of something – in this case natural resources.

Factory ship A large ship that can process whales or fish as the catcher boats bring them in, without having to go back to port.

Fishery The industry of catching, processing and selling fish.

Food chain A natural sequence in which plants are eaten by small animals, which are eaten in their turn by larger animals, which are preyed on by still larger animals.

Habitat The natural home of an animal or plant.

Harpoon A spear that can be thrown or shot at an animal to catch or kill it.

Heavy metals Metals of high density, such as lead or mercury, that are poisonous to people.

Inorganic Made of non-living materials.

Manatee A large sea mammal, sometimes called a seacow.

Migrate To travel regularly from one place to another as the seasons change.

Offal The mostly inedible internal parts of an animal.

Organic Made of, or coming from, living matter.

Parasite An animal or plant that lives on or in the body of another animal, from which it gets food and/or protection without benefiting the host animal.

Pesticide A chemical used to kill creatures that would cause damage to crops.

Plankton The tiny plants and animals that drift in the upper layers of the sea.

Pollutant A substance that causes damage to the environment.

Reclamation The changing of marsh or land covered by water into land suitable for cultivation.

Sand eel A small fish that lives in shallow water.

Snorkeling Swimming underwater, using a tube that extends above the water for breathing.

Sustainable   A catch is sustainable when it leaves enough animals in the wild to breed and replace those that have been caught.

Toxic   Poisonous.

Turbine   A machine that can be turned by the movement of water or steam to generate electricity.

Virus   Minute creatures that cause diseases in plants and animals.

BOOKS TO READ

The Dying Sea by Michael Bright (Watts, 1988)

Endangered Animals by Malcolm Penny (Bookwright, 1988)

The Mysterious Undersea World by Jan L. Cook (National Geographic, 1980)

Oceanography by Martyn Bramwell (Hampstead, 1989)

The Oceans by Martyn Bramwell (Watts, 1987)

The Oceans by David Lambert (Bookwright, 1983)

Our Amazing Ocean by David Adler (Troll Assoc., 1983)

Oil Spills by Joseph Brown (Putnam Pub., 1978)

Saving the Whale by Michael Bright (Gloucester, 1987)

The World's Oceans by Cass R. Sandak (Watts, 1988)

PICTURE ACKNOWLEDGMENTS

Bruce Coleman Ltd. /Gene Ahrens 17 (lower), /B & C Alexander 18, /Jack Dermid 15 (top), /Inigo Everson 21 (top right), /Jeff Foott 10 (lower), 26, /Jennifer Fry 8(lower), / J L G Grande 23 (top), /Leonard Lee Rus 5 (lower), /N R Lightfoot 22, /Fritz Prenzel 27 (top), /William Townsend jnr 25 (top), /Roger Wilmshurst 8 (top), 19 (lower); Oxford Scientific Films /Doug Allan 27 (lower), /Anthony Bannister 29 (lower), /Tony Martin 20, /T C Middleton 24, /Ronald Toms 16, /Charles Tyler 4 (lower), /Kim Westerskov 9 (lower); Planet Earth /Rob Beighton 13 (top right), /J Duncan 5 (top), /Geoff Harwood 13 (lower left), /John Lythgoe 17 (top); Survival Anglia /George Edwards 23 (lower), /Dieter & Mary Plage 21 (lower left), /Annie Price 21 (lower right); Topham cover, iii, 7 (top), 12, 13 (lower right), 14, 29 (top); Wayland Picture library 4, 6,/Shell Photo Service 28; Zefa 7 (lower), 9 (top), 10 (top), 11 (top and lower), 25 (lower).

INDEX